After Reading

After Reading

Poems

Bill Brown

Iris Press
Oak Ridge, Tennessee

Cover and Book Design: Robert B. Cumming, Jr.

Library of Congress Cataloging-in-Publication Data

Names: Brown, Bill, 1948 September 17- author.
Title: After reading : poems / Bill Brown.
Description: Oak Ridge, Tennessee : Iris Press, [2023] | Summary: "During the pandemic Bill Brown started reading friends' poems that he loved. He chose a quote from each poem, and he wrote a tribute poem as a response. That is how this book, After Reading, got its title. Brown selected poems from 33 poets, most of whom he knows and loves as friends" —Provided by publisher.
Identifiers: LCCN 2022055344 (print) | LCCN 2022055345 (ebook) | ISBN 9781604542691 (paperback) | ISBN 9781604548228 (ebook)
Subjects: LCGFT: Poetry.
Classification: LCC PS3552.R68523 A69 2023 (print) | LCC PS3552.R68523 (ebook) | DDC 811/.54—dc23/eng/20221130
LC record available at https://lccn.loc.gov/2022055344
LC ebook record available at https://lccn.loc.gov/2022055345

For my wife, Suzanne—my heart,
my soul, my love

Author Note

During the pandemic I started reading friends' poems that I loved. I chose a quote from each poem, and I wrote a tribute poem as a response. That is how this book, *After Reading*, got its title. I selected poems from 33 poets, most of whom I know and love as friends. Many thanks to KB Ballentine for helping me shape and edit this collection.

—Bill Brown
October 2022

Contents

After Reading "Home"

I drink it like my morning cup of tea.
—Connie Jordan Green

For me it's coffee and a side porch
that often faces deer, mules, horses

and always two cats splayed
on quilted lookouts my wife

surfaced just for them. Acres
and acres of forest and Carolina wrens,

whose voices rule the morning light.
Towhee and thrushes sing in evening shadows,

and always crows at odds with
the sharp-shinned hawks.

Maybe James Taylor, Linda Ronstadt,
or Ella, always Ella,

to replace the news. GrandSally
said hommme, extending the soft "m"

like a hum to start morning tasks,
at night, a blessing, bedtime and book,

a song,
a prayer.

After Reading "Nothing I have"

> *Nothing I have is worth theft of time...*
> —Jeff Hardin

The heart is a clock I need not listen to,
though I often feel it in my temple—

the pulse a little drum to start morning's song,
a closing prayer to night, opening of light

shifting below leaves, a current ripple breeze
on this tiny earth space circling a star.

Morning, Glory, my mother said, seeing
the blue blossoms climbing the drain pipe

on the back porch, my childhood thrown.
Simplicity at hand carves a place for itself.

Beauty is not a commercial. Even Marilyn
Monroe blew snot from her nose.

After Reading "One Morning in Late May"

> *A short life is a long life I could say…*
> —Jeff Hardin

When light rain tops the seeds of hay
    the rain-light lifts the clouds of May

and nothing's coming down Gideon Road
    because a band of crows own it today—

their caws low and personal—the young ones
    learning to peck breakfast from a dead opossum

that lost its life to a thoughtless truck—
    its open stomach a crow gourmet.

Last evening, when an orange-glow-sky
    called for a serenade, wood thrushes

played their flutes to usher in night,
    I thought, *a short life is a long life* today.

After Reading "Approaching October"

I just turned seventy-one and, yes,
    the soul searches years, loves, losses—
all gifts smoothed, circling and sometimes broken.
    The heart, that little muscle, swells

when night birds sing, when morning is opened
    by Carolina wren's chattered song, insistent,
sometimes longing. Today iron weed waves
    its dark purple in the breeze, first day of fall

edging October. A month of longing like April,
    but deeper inside, often a struggle of words
clumped together, not easy to unwind.
    Hummers fight over sugar water on the porch,

a few leaves are turning orange early
    because of drought. A stage is set,
but there's no one to pull the curtains,
    except morning crows and a hopping circle

of buzzards around a dead doe. Will ants
    and field mice eat my dust, will it feed
angelica roots on Roan Mountain Bald,
    or swirl in Tellico River rapids?

Will Christ or Buddha cleanse my soul
    and place it in ground fungus
to house and feed sugar maples
    with the circling of years?

After Reading "The Weight of Snow"

...my soul's silence deepening with fog, with frost, and finally,
with snow.
—KB Ballentine

It was a winter night that silenced my soul,
    a wood stove that brought it back,

my heartbeat a whisper in the dark.
    Our little farm house, four acres,

an orchard, on Crocker Springs Rd.
    Called home from out of town

on New Year's by a neighbor,
    pipes busted, basement flooded,

ice-covered, twenty-one below zero
    in Middle Tennessee. Water turned off,

how something awful can bring you back
    to a self you had forgotten. Waking

in the night to the pop of burning
    oak knots, a cat on each shoulder, night

window a frosted blur, started an inside
    prayer I've never quite silenced—

Jesus, Buddha, Ganesh, Rumi...how can
    terrible lift a heart above the mundane?

Somewhere in a universe filled with billions
    of stars, a voice called out in the darkness

    and I'm almost sure
        it was mine.

After Reading "Prayer"

It is enough to whisper,
until you learn well enough
that there is nothing you need to say
—Susan O'Dell Underwood

The sunrise lighting
   Roan Mountain Bald
      is a silence even wind
         in tall grass can't break.

My tent flap wakes me
   early to rise, stand, listen
      with folded hands on my chest.
         The towhee call that brought

in the night opens the day.
   Morning whispers wordless
      to the lone cloud floating
         like an angel across a blue

the color of my father's eyes.
   Being alone here isn't loneliness.
      A raven in the sky,
         pink rhododendron blossoms

on the ridge
   call out my
      spirit inside.

After Reading "Visitation"

She haunts this empty
space inside me.
—Beto Cumming

When I was seven, mother taught
me to watch cedar waxwings feed
in the mulberry tree. She pointed
out the yellow striped tail, the red
spotted wing, black mask, and tufted crown.
She asked my older sister to explain why
they pass berries down a branch of birds
until all have eaten. Sharing she said—
nature always teaches a lesson—not all
good, like the hawk killing the squirrel,
but they must eat, she said and pointed
to the bacon on our plates.

At sixteen, my father died in my arms.
I lived alone with mother in a big house,
my brothers and sister at college. The empty
space inside me took another turn. I grew
a new identity, lost myself for over a year,
until friends, Bob Dylan and Peter, Paul
and Mary gave me a purpose. Frost and Dickinson
gave me a map—my mother's breakfast prayer
always chimed out Emily's poems.

We lost her in 1995 when she was eighty-four.
Before the funeral I boarded a plane to work
in Idaho. On the long flight, I grieved and traced
my life with her and realized if I could fill
the hollowness inside, I wouldn't—
how wonderfully full emptiness can be.

After Reading "Praying for Freedom"

> *I wonder sometimes on moonless nights*
> *if I can hitchhike on the prayers*
> *of others...*
> —Carol Aronoff

I put out my thumb and a dream-truck pulls over.
  "Where you headed?" he asks
    "Anywhere" I tell him.

So he opens the door, let's me in.
    Soon he pulls in a hardware parking lot,
      and I go in to buy a screwdriver to open

a door in my imagination. A memory
    of a river rises like fog when
      the first fall chill meets water,

and the sound of rapids dancing current,
    a drum roll to greet the mountain forest.
      I breathe in the rich moist air

and say a prayer not to forget
    moments stretched and prolonged
      by the smell of pine needles swelling

at my feet—somewhere in this dream
    I remember my father's voice echoing
    One fine morning when my life is o'er

I'll fly away—and I remember the night
    of his death—how as a kid I wondered
      why God needed him more than we did?

Then an otter emerges in the stream,
    floats on her back to eat a trout.
      I notice a maple tinged with red and think

how nature blossoms a prewinter hope,
    and I think maybe one fine morning
      I'll fly away.

After Reading "Ordinary Heroes"

Dawn yawned the day half awake
—Wesley Sims

Wes, I love your attention to morning birds,
    but of late red-throated hummingbirds
        that lower their pulse close to death at night

have started a war for sugar water on my porch.
    Their iridescent color, needle bills, wing speed
        a blur—*fearless and pugnacious* my field guide reads.

They position themselves in the Rose of Sharon
    and burn more calories chasing each other
        than sharing. Young Carolina wrens hang around

to watch and comment on their lack of civility.
    Jays warn the neighborhood that the sharp-shinned
        hawk is in the air, but hummingbirds don't care.

Who would chase hummers but small hornets
    that drown themselves in feeders adding protein?
        Walk across my porch and become a dart board.

They fly faster than I can duck. Males have a pendulum
    mating dance. All can fly backwards for position.
        Oh, wonder of nature, bring peace to my porch.

Let young females feed. Yes, I put up the feeder.
    Yes, I add more sugar
        to water than is advised.

        I'm guilty, I confess.

After Reading "Static"

My heart lingers, an empty field
—KB Ballentine

October, some fields empty.
Harvest, a religious experience

in rural Tennessee—heart swell
or heart break—rain or lack of.

How landscape shapes the soul,
always present—how deer, crows,

ground hogs and doves harvest
after harvest—how the beginning

of fall splinters something inside
with its glory. Night comes earlier

and a question mark can sit in
the spine like an upside-down hook.

Jesus, Buddha, Ganesh, Rumi—
why does purpose fumble

when autumn night comes,
when first frost turns maple

and sweet gum red?
The creative spirit of the universe

houses billions of stars. The word
"Lord" stayed on my mother's tongue

from first morning to lights-out evening.
Behind my navel where I was

placenta fed in a female pouch,
a praise resides—

my heart lingers,
an empty field.

After Reading "Child on a Balcony"

> *Back streets always have eyes*
> *And yours hold the morning open.*
> —Sandy Coomer

Born on a backstreet in a small southern town,
I opened my eyes when Wags barked. Morning

became the light in maples sifting a breeze
that let in the sun. After breakfast, I climbed

a tree and watched birds and neighbors
start ritual motions of yard and garden work—

waves and howdy-do's, houses close enough
to hear conversations. Early 1950s, war over,

war starting, who's sick, and who will cook
today for old man Williams with tuberculosis?

When it was mother's turn, she let my sister
and me sit on his porch but not enter inside

or get close to the door. There was always
a sense of grief radiating in our parents' eyes

about others' losses—how many folks knocked
on backdoors with green bean casseroles

and always chicken. By early childhood
I knew the family names of every house

on St. John Avenue. With all the sorrow
my world was hop-scotch, water hose battles

and hide and seek. A world of children's hand
prints in wet concrete on our new sidewalk.

At five I knew
        every hand.

After Reading "this is about leaving"

ask me how I am homeless
in my own land.
tell me how
it feels to disappear on your own.
—Lagnajita Mukjhopedhjay

When I watch news and wonder
    about greed and power, about climate
        change making Earth-our-home unlivable

for our children's children's children—
    I lean my ear against an oak root
        and listen. Can rich fungus and dirt,

home to the tree's roots for the gift
    of sugar, tell me about the future.
        When I walk Sulfur Fork Creek

and soak my feet in cool water,
    feel minnows tasting my toes,
        I worship this living clarity,

forget my woes and for a moment
    my name disappears in the current
        helping a willow branch dance

in the sun. I will live on this gift
    of Earth until my life becomes
        a burden, then return to the creative

force, let my bones splinter
    so river otters floating on their backs
        can pick their teeth.

After Reading "Loving Mountains More"

> *Stay longer than a breath, for the mountain*
> *inhales deeper than grass or sand or even bodies*
> *of water*
> —C. Ann Kodra

The wind on Black Balsam Mountain
    makes spicebush swallowtails work

to feed on flowers I love—azalea, laurel,
    rhododendron, bush honeysuckle.

Look across an open bald and just above
    plants, air is dizzy with thousands of butterflies.

Sit on a round stone, cup hands over ears,
    and listen to your breath—draw it in like

the floating miracle around you. Watch
    buntings swirl indigo above blueberries.

Watch bees and hornets get drunk on angelica
    blossoms until they roll on the ground. If you

search the rockfaces geodes will emerge
    and fossils will document creation. Somewhere

in the spirit of lost and found, death and birthing,
    there must be a stillness inside—a kind

of silence my limited
    self can't find.

After Reading "Homemade Coffin"

> *I need no gold to bind me with its weight.*
> *I'll make my journey, weightless, from this land.*
> —C. Ann Kodra

If I were light enough
to walk on water like

a Savior, like a water strider—
if I could float in air like an angel,

or a buzzard rarely flapping a wing—
if I could hang upside down

like a nuthatch—I could leave
this earth where time is based on

particle decay, on night and day.
When the sun, our little star,

peeks in the east, glinting
the tops of trees still shuttered

by night, and one cloud edged
with orange in the breeze,

my spirit, that cartoon bubble
over Pooh's head, could drift

gravity-less from this weighted
gift I have carried with prayer,

sometimes joy, and often
in blue heron dreams.

After Reading "Where I'm From"

I am from the roses in the yard
the tree named after me where
leaves are bigger than my face...
—Caroline

Dear Grand Niece,

After reading your poem,
I realize no one ever named a tree

after me, though in my dreams
I've always wanted to be a sycamore

beside a clear rippling creek—
its white bark splotched

with brown patches reaching
for the sun. In winter, branches'

giant hands with sharp fingers
sharpen the sky's blue. In spring

they often roost great blue herons
whose wings glide through

the forest like kites. The leaves
like tiger paws are bigger than

my face. They float down in fall
to navigate streams, circling

eddies like skiffs. Oh, if my toes
were giant roots in moist earth,

if my fingers could touch the sky.

After Reading "I Once Was Lost"

I lose the thread
of what I'm looking for
as soon as I begin.
—Jeff Hardin

Usually I'm in the closet
   and a thread hanging
      from an old work shirt

I haven't worn in years
   asks me why it's still here.
      The stain on the sleeve

says coffee, red wine,
   but, no, blood—thorns
      from a branch on Roan Mt.,

Appalachian Trail. I rubbed
   the cut with alcohol but
      forgot the band aid

because I couldn't take
   my eyes from a ridge
      covered with gold finches

feeding on thistle, then
   bright indigo from a bunting
      darted into laurel—

my breath caught in my chest
   which suddenly remembers
      why I keep this shirt.

After Reading "Hunkering Down"

> *My bones cannot forget clouded places*
> *of misty days and wind-spirited nights...*
> —Jane Hicks

Winter coming, first morning in the 30s.
   My bones hold me together, cage my heart
      and lungs—still they often seem hollow

when wind in a dance of fall leaves
   whispers secret prayers to a force
      too grand for my little soul. It trails

the years behind, what bones know,
   fingers digiting the maple kitchen table
      just to feel the scars that make it our own.

How leaves palm a night window offer
   a séance of sorts, what mystery the future
      holds for tomorrows to come. A barn owl

speaks its flight song along the forest edge—
   my rib bones feel my breath hold for seconds
      as I imagine its wings moving through oak

and maple to alight on a sycamore branch
   above Sulphur Creek. Everything
      has an ending—the owl's flight,

coming winter,
   even this poem,
      these bones.

After Reading "Night Twins"

The darkness beyond this night window
throws my own face back at me...
—Carol Grametbauer

Ten o'clock, my bedtime—
   checking the doors, I spy
      a neighbor's barn light across
         a field, wonder if a colt is born.

My eyes watch the wonder
   in my eyes mirrored in glass—
      an old scar on my temple
         above my left eye seems larger

than in day time, a boxing injury
   in high school, fifty-five years ago,
      three stitches—how scars take
         us back. I can see contemplation

expressed by my face, pursed lips,
   raised chin, my mother's brown eyes—
      my brown eyes. The barn light's off
         and a flashlight trails the ground

to my neighbor's back porch.
   I click our hall light off and smile
      at a shadowed face as it turns
         toward the bedroom door.

After Reading "The Big Beautiful"

> *Night settled serene and perfect,*
> *Folded me into the big beautiful.*
> —Jane Hicks

The storm ended—a light breeze sang
    rain drops off the porch roof.

Old rockers called us to sit—a soft
    blanket around our shoulders.

At forest edge, a screech owl sang
    a quizzical tune. A fingernail moon

appeared when clouds opened.
    First spring maple leaves, small

and yellow-green, waved like
    timid children before bed.

Somewhere in April darkness,
    rocking quietly together,

        spring spirits crept
           in our heads.

After Reading the Poem "The Light Tears Loose"

The air sparks—
the cosmos no longer contains me
and my soul twists in longing
—KB Ballentine

Early evening and a thrush sings
    the horizon orange, then red

as one bright cloud high in sky
    catches fire—my chest expands

with a breath hard to release
    until a barred owl, early hunting

the shadows, claims territory
    with its ancient yodel. I release

then breathe deep—a mantra
    drawing oxygen from my navel,

my body's imagination, as pin oaks
    rustle a breeze in silence. Silence

isn't possible unless one hears it,
    like a hawk circling high above,

its wings still, a kite flown by a deity.
    The word *soul* appears, more abstract

than heart or mind. Let the coming night
    claim our porch. Rocking chairs

in a breeze, seats for ghosts, invisible
    but rocking, rocking
                in the silence that is.

After Reading "Cenotaph"

My mother and her mother whispered
the words engraved
before us
—Kory Wells

For me, it was on my GrandSally's side.
    Her Grandmother who rode on the back
        of a horse behind her Grandfather from

19th century camp meetings in North Carolina
    to West Tennessee. I have just enough
        Native American genes that she must

have been a half-breed. She sang Cherokee
    lullabies to my GrandSally as a child.
        Her dark-skinned picture was destroyed

during Civil Rights by some bigot cousin.
    I'm the only child in my family with dark skin.
        One summer, 1969, I worked construction

in the sun and turned so brown a woman
    in the grocery asked me what race I was.
        I have crossed the Trail of Tears many times—

my shoulders tense, my breath tight. More
    than 4,000 men, women, and children
        lost their lives—*nunahi-duna-dlo-hilu-l*

means *Trail where they cried.* Hiking
    above Bald River Falls, I found
        sites where Monroe County

Cherokee buried their relatives' dust in
    shallow graves. I thought how Ball River
        must be a sacred stream. I dropped

to my knees, read their names
    out loud as a prayer—the soil
        pressed inward to my bones.

After Reading "Last Swallow of Light"

> *Let moonlight silver my face*
> *let emptiness finally fill the rest of me—*
> —KB Ballentine

Emptiness can fill me—how the moon
and twinkle of stars open a night porch

with faces—sometimes maple leaves'
flutter become sleepy breathing

of dead parents—how sounds in
nature mimic the living even when

they're gone. As a boy my bedroom
lay between my sister's and parents.

Breathing often orchestrated my dreams,
like trees in a dark wind move my hands

to my ears to discern whose face, whose
bright eyes emanate from natural sounds—

perhaps through memory, emptiness opens
a space for joy, sorrow's cousin—both born

by caring. Tonight, a great horned owl's
territorial chant echoes at forest edge.

My past hunts as well—sprinkled
with moonlight in trees.

After Reading "Walking Boundaries"

Night weavers hang prisms...
—Jane Hicks

A thousand rainbows
   greet the morning sun,
      spiders' gift to Bob's

Bald above Tellico.
   A light breeze ripples
      color as if a deity might

take up a new home,
   and me, just a pilgrim
      on this journey, inherits

holy bliss. Imagine how
   Monet might fit this
      on canvas. But when

dew dries and colors fade,
   I'll count on my dreams
      to explain what I witnessed,

use it as a beauty crutch
   to lean on, when I return
      to a world I don't seem

      to often know.

After Reading "Available Light"

*The things I want are simple too—a fingerprint
on the window of understanding, a thread of faith.*
        —Sandy Coomer

A heartbeat that doesn't
    start in my temple,

a breath of air deep
    in my lungs,

my fingers shaped by
    descendants of family,

formed new and spry,
    my calloused heels

moon-shaped and smooth,
    my navel remembering

my mother—warmth inside
    another body,

your chin resting
    on a pillow beside me,

night, a prayer whispered
    by wind in maples,

a hilltop pond dancing
    the moon—

whippoorwill
    towhee echo

wood thrush
    harmonious

After Reading "I Mark this Gone Place
with Foxfire"

> *I find a poplar stump, sit against its damp wood,*
> *breathe deep and imagine apple blossoms,*
> *patches of pennyroyal, hillsides unvanished*
> —Lisa J. Parker

Not all that vanishes will return—rivers
    killed by coal acid, mountain creeks poisoned
with bauxite deposits unearthed by building

roads in Cherokee Forest—what humans
    touch for money, convenience—
what the future, if there is one, loses

from us. I sit on an oak stump on North River
    near Tellico and watch swallowtails flit
above spice bushes and feed on bear scat

in the road. I used to fish a native trout stream
    near. The trout are gone now. Dick and I
backpacked up the stream, witnessed

a bear fight, heard a golden eagle scream
    above Bob's Bald. Dick said we'd catch
native trout for supper, the limit's three,

but let's keep two and eat beans if we're
    hungry. His honesty, his love of nature,
a practiced religion. Now the creek is dead

and Dick died of sudden cancer. I said
    goodbye to him near his blessed cabin,
as a barred owl uttered its musical *whoo,*

    whoo, above the campfire
      we loved
        to stoke.

After Reading "Chewing on the Dead"

"Poem," I told her this afternoon, "I've got to quit
talking to dead people."
—Alice Sandford

"It's whether or not you expect them to talk back,"
    my dead mother said. It was her quizzical voice,
        the one that she used watching eagles fish

at Reelfoot Lake. And even though she was blind
    in one eye, she could point out their flight
        from Big Island before I caught the moving dot

that became a white head and tail. Sometimes
    it would catch a fish too big to fly, but the lake
        had stumps from its primal forest before the New

Madrid earthquake formed the wilderness
    of open water and swamp. Talking to the dead
        out loud can get one in trouble. Say I'm in a fish

market and sniff the air, tell my mother it isn't
    fresh and the owner kicks me out. So supper is
        peanut butter sandwiches. She says that's better

than old fish and I agree. The best thing about
    talking to the dead—if I pour her a glass of wine,
        I get to drink it—of course, that ends our conversation.

After Reading "How to Find the Center of a Circle"

> *...was called a nigger*
> *g sounds,*
> *around my neck*
> *like white spiders*
> *a carousel of hate.*
> —Tiana Clark

TC,

In 1955 I was seven years old,
living in West Tennessee, white only
    water fountains, white only, white
only everything. Barbara, Linda Jo

and I were playing chase in yards
on St. John Ave. We noticed
    a black man doing hard, persistent
yardwork all day long. He smiled

at us when we laughed or squealed.
The end of the day came and we
    found him sitting on the sidewalk,
his feet in the street, head in hands,

weeping. A cantaloupe sat beside him,
and he kept saying "a cantaloupe,
    a day's work for a cantaloupe—
what will my children eat?"

We ceased our play and walked
quietly home. 64 years ago and I
    never forgot his hands, his shaking
shoulders, his voice.

After Reading "Scouting the Color Wheel in Winter"

The sky after a cold front passes through,
the color of eternity.
—Carol Grametbauer

A long cloud, high, separated like
    a hunting eagle's wing—somewhere
in subconscious edge of daydreams,

a story hides. Which consonant, noun,
    verb will start it—is a coin toss
seldom ready to land. Colors emerge

as our star gets ready for bed—a child
    appears at a sunset window, coaches
the old man to un-clinch his fist

and start with home—the porch
    rocker, wind-rocking, his mother's
voice finds a ballad, his father's

tenor, her heart full with two young
    sons, while he is on a battle ship, WWII.
What validates this collage but

the holy palace of memory—two more
    children are born after his safe return.
Sister and little brother enter stage left

and start their morning play, dancing
    up and down the stairs, singing
their father's favorite song.

After Reading "Dust"

> *a bridge to where night*
> *dripped like fire when the rains still came.*
> —Jane Hicks

The bridges in one's life are uncountable
    like the images the soul creates
        to explain them—

a fire dripping,
    a crop saving rain,
        a phone call

of a mother's death,
    a dog's last howl
        at the moon.

Bridges
    Bridges
        Bridges

that must be crossed
    if life goes on,
        if a heart stops beating.

A fog filled night
    crossing over a river—
        how slow can one go

without stopping,
    what we imagine
        might come toward us,

even when it doesn't,
    and we hear our own sigh
        on the other side.

After Reading "After A While I Just Got Up and Took A Walk"

...to be among tall grasses nuzzling light...
—Jeff Hardin

is a church of sorts—tall blades,
    like fingers, like knives, sharpening
        in the air, forming silent prayers

toward morning, toward night.
    Our sun or moon or distant stars
        cuddle a close arrangement

of wordless psalms—not wishing
    to claim credit or change beliefs
        in the endless moments uncounted

to the sky—hear whispers...
    the whispers...
        whispers.

After Reading "Damasked Sky"

Pied, Stippled, Demasked.
The sky mirrored in the lake...
—Elizabeth Howard

I come here to write too—
  maybe not your lake but
    ripple, reflection, bejeweled
      with light speckled by swirl
        of leaves. No snow yet, but
a chill. My shoulders wish
  to be held—a self-hugging
    afternoon. The pen in my
      pocket isn't sure it needs
        removing, but I brought
gloves once worn by a
  dead friend. Somehow his
    memory brings back a boy-
      hood I wouldn't still have
        if he hadn't joined it—
a small flock of wood ducks
  circles, reaches out webbed feet
    to land—reds and greens brighten
      a world settling for winter.
        The ink in my pen loosens
with memory, to see Ship's
  white-blond hair, his old jeep,
    the sparkle of campfires caught
      in the lake's flapping darkness,
        wavetops catching the flames' glow.
Today, I will celebrate the dead,
  the living—let the sky reflection,
    wood-violet blue, creep into my words—
      help them dance with sparkling light,
        pray the lap and splash of water

          follow me to my grave.

After Reading "Gull River"

> *My hopes worm their way into the apple*
> *where all my yesterday's rust.*
> —Noel Conneely

No surprise, so many poems written
    about rivers—their current streams

like our subconscious all night to make
    meaning, perhaps, of yesterday's

whispers of sleeping childhood,
    first snow, first violent storm sat out

in a basement, wind and thunder
    swimming the trees. A teen dreams

of a lover's arms, wakes, remembering
    a face he's never seen. The older we get

our dead appear, always our dead, how
    we learn to let go by holding on.

River, we can always see our faces
    in your water's surface. This morning

memory's beard turned from brown
    to gray, surrounded by white, still

floats with rotten birch leaves stored
    in eddies, to be released like a soul

slipping out the edge back into
    a movement always downstream,

past sycamores reaching above laurel
    with white fingers.

After Reading "Cenotaph"

When my mother
was in her mother's womb
I was there too, beginning
—Kory Wells

How many infants can follow
    from one mother's womb—
my DNA has many more Neanderthal

traits than most—cross Africa through
    Israel, through Greece into central Europe
to the British Isles. My mother's mother,

dead before my birth, but my grandfather,
    my name sake, lived till I was three
and held me in his stroke muted hands.

Dead some 24 years, my mother's
    brown eyes stare back from my mirror.
I claim them from her womb, along

with my penchant for gardening,
    Ella Fitzgerald, and white bean soup.
When we ate fried chicken, Sunday lunch,

mother picked back and wings so we
    could have more meat. As a child,
a drum stick held in my hand

was the Holy Grail. My mother
    appears in my dreams—her beautiful
smile, her stern frown, her whispers

about roses, her Jesus, my father's
    tenor in the shower. One night not
long ago, I awoke in warm, sweet,

darkness, the sound of my pulse
    augmented by a stronger beat—a fetal
dream inside a body, the dream

    I wish to die in.

After Reading "Augury"

Because bones are minerals inside the catacombs,
there is wind inside the bone.
—Michelle Poulos

The first wind-bone experience came
    one afternoon in the Sawtooth Mountains.

10,000 feet, snow-spotted in July, entered
    my navel like nurture, rose through ribs

into throat, crowned my skull, eyes
    a blur of wonder. Something, inside,

dreamlike, speaks mortality/immortality,
    either Holy. Later it rose from my sore

ankles into my knees, said I was alive
    and the silver clouds circled over

the Salmon River
    like a golden eagle's eyes.

After Reading "Pause"

*The lapse is a pause on the stair
where you've forgotten from which direction
you've come.*
—Michelle Poulos

The direction a loved
    one's death gives you—

a mirror with your mother's
    eyes still in your eyes—tears

collect on your chin, drip
    little rivers down your

Adam's apple. Unbutton
    your shirt, see if they can

reach your navel where
    her body, your home,

fed you into life.
    Turn on the stairs

where a night window
    finds a shadow

    of her face.

After Reading "Why wherever you stand is home:"

ode to owning all along (everything and nothing) all at once
—Lagnajita Mukhopadghyay

This is my hand   this my foot

My hand that fingered   the first doorknob

To open   the foot that stood

On the last step   to leave

How many doors   how many steps

So many leavings   and arrivals

One life   reads

From my navel   being clipped

After I escaped   my blessed mother

To my ashes being cast   off Balsam Mountain

Dear Jesus, Buddha,   Ganesh, Rumi

Teach me how to own   a life that I will lose

Help my hands shape   something, someone,

Worth   loving

Sycamores beside   Sulphur Creek

Let minnows   swim their roots   to feed

What will I create   for others

What hymn   to sing

What poem   of gratitude

Can form   unsigned

Anonymous   as prayer

After Reading "Offering"

> *Or is it once again love's clumsy sacrifice*
> *the restless heart lifting up its raucous music,…*
> —Harry Moore

Oh pileated, redheaded, downy, hairy—
  the woodpeckers of my childhood,
    my adulthood, offering up a drum,

heaven made, even for an insect serving.
  We all must eat, but few drum our meals
    into existence, taking the rotten wood on

our roof for breakfast, nature's alarm clock,
  like my mother's *Wakeup, Lazy Bones.*
    When I was restless as a child, Uncle Tom

called me peckerwood. I always considered
  that slur an honor. Somewhere in the raucous
    Nature of Nature, creation takes of life's

music, teaches existence's rhythm.
  At the lakeside where the rolling song
    of kingfisher closes with sundown's

surface feeding, a drum on a dead
  sycamore stump
    brings in the night.

After Reading "Deus Absconditis"

> *One day God moved out, vanished like*
> *deadbeat dad on the run leaving*
> *an empty sky.*
> —Harry Moore

No one seemed to notice until
    prayers quit healing the sick,
        more animals got run over by cars,

the green grass earth worships
    began to brown, trout streams
        filled with leeches to suck

fishermen's blood, vultures
    became our national bird, started
        eating bald eagles, leaving

the dead to rot, infesting the air.
    Even the Central American children
        caged on the border by our government

abandoned the desire for freedom
    and prayed, instead, for death.
        So many politicians were

dearly happy, thankful that God
    moved out, and the empty sky
        filled with burning coal and gas—

        even Satan couldn't breathe.

After Reading "A Short Distance From Mountains"

The truth is half a day can pass with nothing more than the scent
of honeysuckle before approaching rain...
—Jeff Hardin

Is the scent of honeysuckle truer
                  when rain approaches

Is rain that can't find a place
                  to fall truer than a downpour

Is the creative spirit that gives
                  honeysuckle rain, as well as

a scent that romances the nose
                  and draws bees to feed

as true as my mother's womb
                  that brought three brothers
and a sister to this little planet

Are we as holy as being born
                  in a barn in Bethlehem

Are such questions as unanswerable
                  as honeysuckle, rain, the sound
of wind in spring oak leaves

After Reading "Requiem"

But nothing, silence: only, among her things,
this picture of her at twenty...
—Harry Moore

Her hair was blonde, eyes brown,
   lips pursed in a gentle smile.
      When her infant was born dead,

she carried it for her friends
   to see how beautiful she was.
      Then the infection in her uterus

found her in a time with no
   penicillin, and sulfur couldn't
      do the job. She joined her baby

in the old cemetery where her
   parents would one day find
      themselves. The aunt I never

knew—except how my mother
   still mourned her sister's too
      soon departure, long before

I was born. We brought a little
   girl angel to grace her stone.
      If I could have watched her

eyes sparkle, perhaps justice
   could find something to blame
      on one side of the grave.

After Reading "Detachment"

Sit
still in the center of the room and just breathe,
and feel the grinding
without trying to change it
—Kate Daniels

Change is a strange concept
in winter, in summer, when
every day has a different number
but the cold, the heat continues
the same until spring, until fall

The grinding   the grinding

Hope enters in small measures,
like tree roots feeding fungi
bits of sugar for giving them
a home, like maple seeds
coptering away to find birth
if soil and moisture

Provide   provide

Can morning coffee and evening
wine help us live day by day
on a little planet

spinning   spinning

Can creatures live a life without
making, hopefully, beauty, meaning?
Does a dragonfly consider a life other
than feeding and crapping—its flight,
remarkable, its shining wings, rainbows
in the light

questions   questions

Sit still in the middle of the room

Abide   abide

After Reading "Walking With Lightning Bugs"

A thin slice of moon shines between the limbs of the tree
and lightning bugs join the stars.
—Mary Thom Adams and Helen Lewis

Inside my dream a *slice of moon* comforts
   the evening star as a lightning bug swirl

climbs through laurel to meet the sky—
   to watch the moon's reflection in moist

green leaves, petite heavens glinting
   in a mountain breeze. I wake to write

this image down before it's lost in dreams.
   A barred owl claims the night with its somber song.

A shooting comet burns in darkness before
   lost in earth's domain, a little trail, then

nothing but distant stars. Years back before
   night hawks didn't return one spring, *chuck*

wills widow echoed through the orchard,
   their courting songs. Now only tree frogs

and toads harmonize night. Morning
   opens echoing Carolina wrens who

    poke their beaks in every critter's business.

After Reading "Church"

> *There will never be again an ear*
> *more willing than that wild, wild field.*
> —Susan O'Dell Underwood

How many *wild fields* have I worshiped in—
    uncountable, but always wind in tall grass,
        swallowtails dancing over honeysuckle,
            gold finches and blue birds feeding

on thistle, on a gnat hatch, to the applaud
    of crows, of ravens. One finds herself
        on knees, whispering without words
            to something holy as living. The evening

song of towhees signaling a closing day,
    the door song of coming night, mauve
        clouds turning blue, then gray. Worship
            is not defined, confirmed by temples,

by pulpits—but by one's breath, heartbeat,
    blood flow, a temple-pulse a dreamer
        wakes to, an acoustic arrangement—self—
            life—anonymous—always fleeting.

After Reading "With a Thousand-Tongued Hunger"

My brother's hands made small fires
that would rise in the darkness
                        —Kory Wells

near Price's Pond where often
        an orange flame caught water's surface

with its light and movement.
        Our little scout cooking dishes

dismantled to heat soup, chili
        or stew—the spark and crackle

of burning oak filled our spirits
        as well as our famished stomachs.

Barred owls circled our camp
        upon hearing my brother's hooting,

letting the sound caress
        the back of his throat into a mountain

yodel. Some nights among the floating
        sounds of owls searching for this new

stranger, a few coyote howls rose
        to a full moon, chilling our shoulders

like the cold I wake to some nights
        to owl hoots and dream my brother's

hands cradling a little flame, his fingers
        as gentle as cuddling an infant child.

After Reading "The Question of Where"

You had been so present,
how could you be gone, and to where—
—Connie Jordan Green

An empty room is crowded
by a lack of presence, chairs,
coffee table like the portrait

of a grandmother, stare out
at nothing, barely acknowledge
light drifting behind

the window's pulled shade.
A dripping faucet tries its best
to fill the silence but only

proves the absence, and you,
who is not an "I" or "me"
or "third person," must be

where herons float through
sycamores like angels—not
an Icarus flying toward the sun,

not a Mary Magdalene, spiritually
seduced by Christ, but wren songs
to celebrate another earth day where

the where has lost its meaning,
and mourning doves pray to be
spelled, morning.

After Reading "No Believer"

...I wake
to find myself older than I can understand
With most of my life in a fragment that only I remember...
—W.S. Merwin

My fragments...at 19 getting sunburned in Arizona
on the way to my hippy commune days in California,
skin peeling off my face, no money for healing cream,
little for food...

My Fort Knox days... at 21, my young wife visiting me
after months apart, in a cheap motel in Kentucky,
so in love...

...Crashing down a class four rapid in an open canoe,
thinking a friend was waving me forward, but was
telling me not to come...

...killing a six-foot rattlesnake in my yard so it wouldn't
bite my neighbor's dog...

...Finding our first yellow lady's slipper on a trail in
North Carolina mountains, my wife holding her fingers
over her mouth, a prayer of joy...

My 18-year-old tabby dying in my wife's arms, knowing
from his face, he knew she was holding him...

...Showing up a moment after a close friend's death, lying
in bed hugging his body with his wife...

When does blood run cold, run hot...when do fragments
race or slow your temple's pulse? ...at my age, thankful
for every beat, drop by drop....

After Reading "To Paula in Late Spring"

Let me imagine that we will come again
When we want to and it will be spring
—W.S. Merwin

And the first yellow-billed cuckoo will arrive
    from the Caribbean as a rain crow and sing

what's coming with us from its hollow
    pronouncements in the hickory crown.

The whippoorwills call from
    ground nests hidden in last fall's leaves.

The hermit thrush ushers in evening
    with its mating call, and we mate again

with these sounds that brought us kicking
    in the first world outside our mothers,

weeping and cooing to bribe God into
    letting us back in, our navels attached.

After Reading "Place"

On the last day of the world
I would want to plant a tree
　　　　　　　—W.S. Merwin

Not a cedar or a pine that keeps green
　　all winter, but a sycamore, its January

white-mapped bark, snow-like, its seeds
　　clinging to limbs, ready to fly the breeze

to plant anew. On the last day of the world
　　I would throw rocks in a passive stream,

not heavy clunks, but thin circles
　　that skip across water getting baptized

before they reach the furthest shore.
　　On the last day, let me search under

logs to find skinks with tails that fall
　　off and wiggle, attracting predators

as lizards escape. On the last day let
　　my spirit come to silence, as mauve

clouds decorate our sun's last
　　setting before the certain freeze.

After Reading "A Given Day"

I am home it is coming back to me I am
Remembering the gradual sweetness of morning
                                    —W.S. Merwin

Without understanding
  without wishing
    to understand
      a timelessness at my feet
        longed for
      when waking
    to a sleeping wife
  at my side
her newly curled
  blonde hair
    flaming the pillow
      below her cheek
        her chin

    an old girl cat
  at my feet
named Cecelia
stretches all four legs
    at once
      whispering something feline
        that I from experience
        understand

      Carolina wrens
      announce a new day
      as if creation
      can begin again
      without the Milky Way's
    permission or care

After Reading "Lately When Sorrows Come"

> *Some days the sky is so full of sorrows*
> *they could be mistaken for shadows unnamed*
> —Susan Laughter Meyers

a crow with a broken wing—

a fawn hidden in tall grass
waiting for the doe that
can't return—

an infant in an abandoned car
in the Walmart parking lot—

an old woman in a nursing home
hugging Raggedy Ann—

a kitten in the top of a tree—

where is the wind when
sycamore seeds need to fly—

where is the rain on a scorched
field of corn—

when the barred owl leaves
the barn mow hole at night
which baby rabbit in the litter—

which mole above ground—
all the living must eat, drink
or die—

can the sound of leaves at a night
window be a symphony without
a coming storm—

can sunlight on the porch heat
the wooden floor for the cat
waiting, waiting at the door—

would you let a child put
a plastic flower on a grave—

After Reading "The Speed of Light Is Constant"

> *yet, the weight of earth*
> *is so much less than that of grief*
> —John Mannone

Sometimes a heart beat
is an acoustical arrangement
of sorrow, a composition

in a minor key allowing
a slow awkward breathing.
Standing at my Father's grave

at 16, standing at his grave
at 71—rubbing his veteran's
tombstone like his hand petted

the spaniels' that worshiped him.
I remember, as a teenager, how
my cousins wondered why

I couldn't cry, as if my tears
might justify grief—as if sobs
always followed tense aching

shoulders, tired eyes from staring
at the night ceiling until a dream
crept in and a series of images—

tending a night camp fire, rowing
a fishing boat, the sound of owls
hunting, then waking to a morning

to find mourning instead. At 71
my grief is a form of love. I still
remember the healing of his touch,

his beautiful tenor in the shower,
singing sometimes at night for mother
as I pretended to sleep.

After Reading "Arguing with the Buddha"

> *Quick dip and flicker-fall of cardinal's wings,*
> *Skeleton-webs of leaves that float, fly, fling…*
> —Alice Sandford

Your words create a moving painting
   in my dreams—nature's movement

that might delay decay until the fungus,
   among us, starts it back again. So life

continues with and without our presence,
   and *the shifting dart of light* from

dead stars help March tulips bloom
   red, mauve, yellow, blue.

Perhaps the last frost will burn blossom
   edges before April sings with towhees

and irises unfold, orchid-welcomes
   to redwing blackbirds, home again,

   home again, home again.

After Reading "The Next Poem..."

The next poem I write
will open a door where I find myself.
—Beto Cumming

In a closet
    in Plato's Cave,

not the shadows
    on the wall

lit by fires
    to my strapped selves

but a small peephole
    open to the unknowable

like fungi in my yard
    that outnumber stars.

Socrates, what
    does "Pure Form"

mean and why
    can't I imagine it?

Self, stand
    at the peephole,

pretend you're
    Jonah in a whale,

or gas in a bowel
    longing to escape.

After Reading "Poem 24"
from *Love and Other Hungers*

Nobody passes the plate for birdsong, surely.
This singing is bread and honey enough...
—Susan O'Dell Underwood

Susan,

Carolina wrens voice
    our wakeup calls,

a trill, an echo,
    before the towhee sings

drink-your-tea at forest edge.
    A hand-full of cardinals

flirt in early spring, never
    knowing how they complete

our world. Chickadee dee dee
    on the old swing set where

our feeders hang
    with suet and seed.

Flit of titmouse,
    upside-down spider-walk

of nuthatch on
    tree bark, and never

enough symphonic
    wood thrush,

hermit thrush
    lowering the sun.

After Reading Poem "8"
in *Love and Other Hungers*

> *Think: How many birds singing you will never hear.*
> —Susan O'Dell Underwood

Walking through a local forest
I notice many fallen, uprooted trees—

some over a hundred years old.
I start their stories in my head,

last November's tornado, terrible
straight-line winds, perhaps their

time to die and start again new-life.
But how to make up bird songs

I never hear has me stuck in a dreamless
world that silence wrens calling

each other in the rose of Sharon,
or in the honeysuckle beside

the horse pasture, where mules beg
for apples and dance to crow calls.

After Reading "Among the Unseen"

...and night spreads like a moth
settling her soft wings.
—Connie Jordan Green

Luna,
Polyphemus,
Achemon Sphinx moth—

how on my childhood porch
I found you still sleeping on
screen and always on backyard
maple bark, before you

disappeared into your day world.
Many Native Americans
consider moths a symbol
of transformation, healing

and prayer. Moth cocoons
were used as sacred rattles.
Other tribes believe moths
are kin to death and ghosts,

that may bring messages
from the spirit world.
190 million years on earth—
what spirit designed

such grace and beauty—
each sighting a gift
of living prayer.
Oh, if all nights

could settle soft,
soft wings.

After Reading "Let the Words Fall Where They May"

Let the Words come like an ache
Moving through my timid hand...
—Rita Sims Quillen

If only I could get them loose—
like prints on my fingertips—
line-filled and wordless. Ache
must come first as words fall out,
pronouncing themselves like
waking dreams. And story finds
itself with the muse sitting beside
an old spotted hound who *does*
his business (Granny says) too
close to the turnips. Then place—
orchard, pond, fence lined with
honeysuckle, trimmed graveyard
across from Bible Hill Baptist,
crucifix raising out of the roof.
And always the ghost at sunset
hovering over graves as women
collect dry clothes from back-yard
lines. I was a child sitting at the
kitchen table, where Granddaddy
said *children sit quiet and let*
adults talk. So I learned to listen
and later the words collected
in my *timid hand,* from ache,
love, and always wonder to find
a spring where we drank from a gourd.

After Reading "The Dream"

I was not
done with my sorrow after all.
—Andrea Potos

Sorrow, like a ghost, sits on my shoulder,
   whispers *don't pretend I'll ever leave.*
      Love drives a slow boat in waves, tries

to stay afloat, to carry on life with grief.
   Our dead keep their names in carved marble—
      Paleozoic rock as old as 542 million years.

My father died at 57, my mother at 84,
   At 71, why would I wish to let them go?
      In the mirror I find my mother's brown eyes.

My father's, October-sky-blue are my
   brother's. Somewhere a girl dreams
      a dead pet returning—wakes to the joy

of dog—his bad breath, his licking tongue
   on her cheek. Then he's gone again—
      the little grave dug with her father beside

her mother's roses. The dead live with me—
   ask why I'm so concerned. Somewhere
      in the drift of clouds their spirits hover—

their voices fade close to my ears,
   a silence-heart-ache turns into a songless
      song, a hum at the edge of breath.

After Reading "Mom, Leaving"

...she
turned to enter her next
story we have no language for.
—Andrea Potos

We will all
    enter that
        next story,

a dream
    in which
        silence

decorates
    night stars,
        and wind drifts

through maple
    leaves with
        no sound.

After Reading "A Transplant Leaves Minnesota, 1973"

...turned toward the hills
that give me help, that give me shelter
hold the sky where it belongs.
—Jane Hicks

How hills hold
the sky with their palms

and fingering trees—
and the sky rests

its boneless sighs
in peace.

A child
at a morning window

stretches her arms,
puts her hands

behind her neck
and pretends

her shoulders
are the hills

that hold
the Milky Way together

like dark matter,
as the young sun peeps

through gathering blue
to hover its fire.

After Reading "Some Houses"

> *...the ground*
> *in our wake, glowing*
> *in the dim light*
> *of ancient stars.*
> —Carol Grametbauer

An ancient farmhouse in my childhood
is still *glowing in the dim light of ancient stars.*

65 years ago, age five, my dreamworld memory
still walks the small steps up to an open porch.

The crow of rooster and chattering hens gobbling
what's left of breakfast scattered in the yard.

Evening—ghosts in the cemetery by the church—
always whippoorwills and barn owls.

I wake this morning beside my wife and let
the old house drift back—its spirit poses a question—

Why, it asks? I rise, turn on coffee and watch
our sun shifting tree shadows in the yard.

Shadows maybe—shadows of an old man
drinking from a spring with a gourd, shadows

of a billy-goat beard hanging over a fence
by the barn, shadows of four pallbearers

carrying a homemade cedar casket
from the little church.

After Reading "Anticipation"

> *The black-capped chickadee sings*
> *the ache of the sea and approaching spring.*
> —KB Ballentine

At 71, ache is a word that finds my shoulders,
   my lower back. The sea created, nurtured
      and lost lives for millions of years. It must

ache as it once again introduces Spring.
   The morning chickadee song wakes me
      to the warmth of my wife. A light frost

at the end of March trims grass blades
   in the sun, blue violet buds are forming
      in the yard. A piliated woodpecker drums

a maple, sets a cadence for morning,
   a feeding drumbeat before breakfast.
   First light burns light green of leaves

beginning to form. Somewhere in my heart's
   closet t-shirts hang with empty pockets.
      I pull a grey one over my head and start anew.

Carolina wrens begin building a new nest
   in a basket on the porch wall. The sea,
      a universe itself, continues to ache as it must.

After Reading "My Heart's Erratum"

My longing shadow's dark substratum
Addendum to my phantom selves...
—E.P. Fisher

My shadowed lives whisper to me
About deaths I've lived before my death.
Mother and father, kin and friends...
Yet I'm still here watching green leaves
Announce June, listening to wood thrushes
Sing in another evening. Somewhere
In the closing orange of sunset, my name
Gets lost as the mantra of wind in trees
Says earth to me, says earth. Even when
My selves sit at the edge of daydreams
On an afternoon porch, fuss of Carolina wren
Or *drink-your-tea* of towhee, pull me
To this waking world. In the back yard
Under a rotten log, a ring-neck snake
swallows a worm, a wood beetle
eats its home. So what is home and can
we carry place with us?

      I would like to age
With the sounds of earth giving its moments
Down our daily journey, realizing that Thoreau
And Emerson carried place deep inside and wouldn't
Pretend to know what an existential tick of a clock
Really means, except an ending we call death
Is always out there—not a skeleton face, ghost-
White, but...a coming and leaving, a coming
And leaving...and being awake enough

        To listen...

After Reading "Reality"

*Sooner or later,
that old curmudgeon,
reality, settles
into your recliner,...*
—Lola White

pets the cat and listens to death
hovering in the maple leaves—

is it yours—death can't say—
it's just listening to chipping sparrows

flitting about, full of life. Death
acts tired, too often feared, seldom

honored—sometimes has a chip
on its shoulder, but not this morning,

when wrens enjoying spring snack
on a hatch of gnats. Reality changes

so often, it doesn't understand time—
a mini-second as full as an hour, sub-

particles dancing with sub-sub-particles
underneath my toenails, on the tip

of my nose. Somewhere in Africa
a mother elephant circles a baby born

too soon—its blank eyes stare up
toward a dying star we call our sun.

Such quiet weeping, death thinks,
such smothering
                sorrow.

After Reading "How Long"

> *...until the wind*
> *should call us forth to cross*
> *the gulfs between the stars.*
> —W. Luther Jett

Four hundred billion stars
float the Milky Way like
sub-particles beneath leaves
in a Tennessee forest.
Our dust, eternal and rich,
will fill and sometime
build on whatever
of existence in its sacred,
nameless forms of forms
of forms.

Yet,

this morning at first light,
our little sun calls us
to wake, to usher in
a February day with a porch
lined with sunflower seeds
to feed gold and purple
finches who line tree limbs
in winter cold. How long
can an old man complete
this holy task, how long?

After Reading "Balance"

The ear that hears wind scatter in cedar
woods listens also to the earth curve
beneath your foot.
—Floyd Skloot

It is not exactly a sound
    but a silent speed, motion

erased by powers beyond us
    while oak leaves flutter

in a breeze, and a squirrel
    buries an acorn for winter.

Somewhere in the pulse
    a finger feels a heartbeat

when it touches a wrist
    while a comet flashes Mars

with its trailing breath.
    Dear Wonder, forgive our

attention span in this miracle.
    Earth teach us to kneel

in a garden and plant seeds
    as a prayer. Help it to grow

so we can grow. Let our short
    lives become a garden.

Bill Brown is the author of twelve poetry collections and a writing textbook, *Important Words*, on which he collaborated with Malcolm Glass. In 1999 Brown wrote and co-produced the Instructional Television Series, *Student Centered Learning*, for Nashville Public Television. Brown directed the writing program at Hume-Fogg Academic High School in Nashville for 19 years. His philosophy that those who write live more examined lives fostered a love of words in generations of students. He retired from Hume-Fogg in May 2003 and accepted a part-time lecturer's position at Peabody College of Vanderbilt University. In 1995 the National Foundation for Advancement in the Arts named him Distinguished Teacher in the Arts. He has been a Scholar in Poetry at the Bread Loaf Writers Conference, a Fellow at the Virginia Center for the Creative Arts, and a two-time recipient of Individual Artist Fellowships in poetry from the Tennessee Arts Commission. In 2011 the Tennessee Writers Alliance awarded Brown Writer of the Year. He continues to do consultant work and lead writing workshops.